AN ACCOMPLISHED LIFE

NON FICTION POETRY ALONG WITH REALISTIC EVENT

AASHI PRIYA

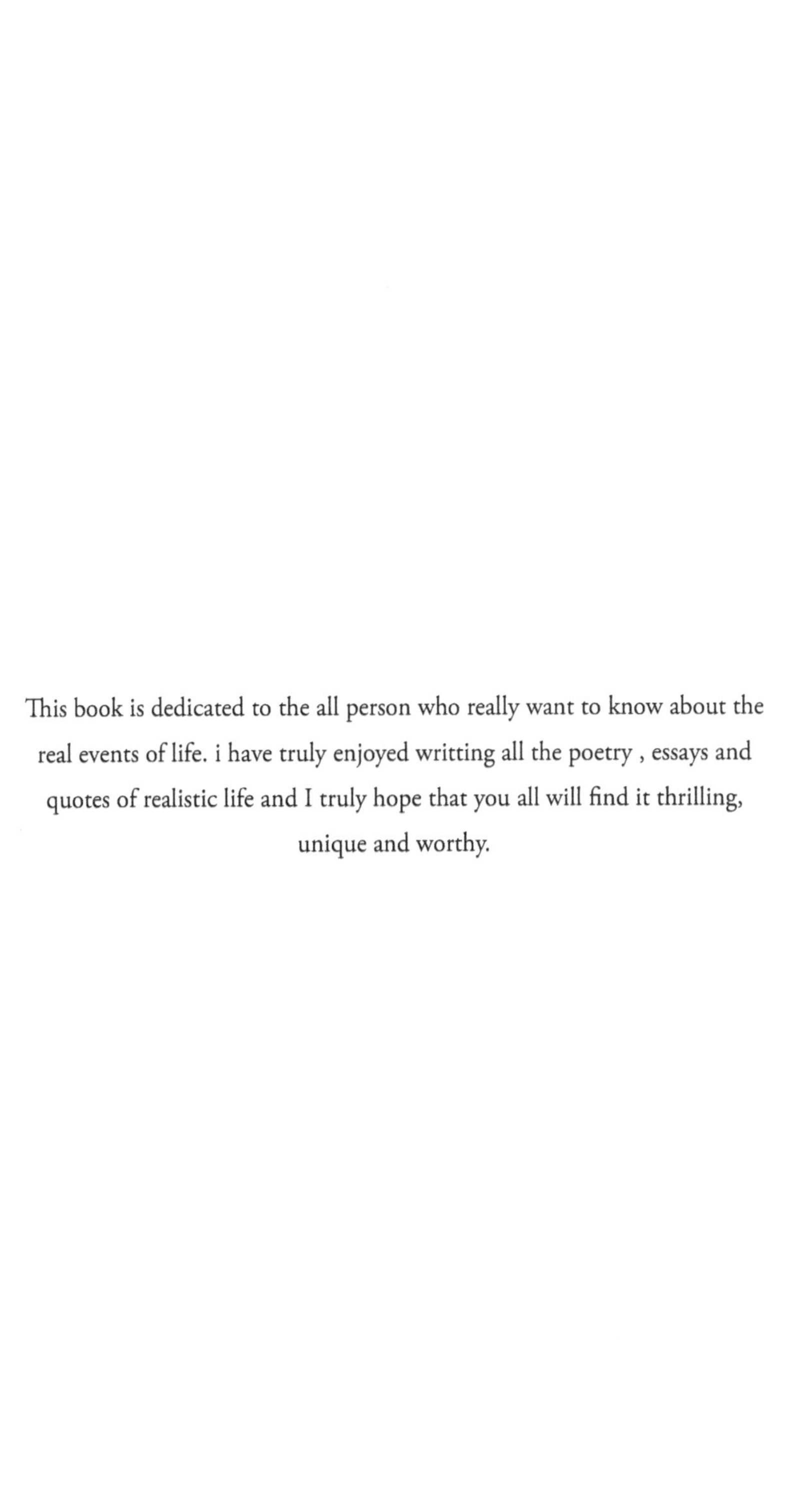

This book is dedicated to the all person who really want to know about the real events of life. i have truly enjoyed writting all the poetry , essays and quotes of realistic life and I truly hope that you all will find it thrilling, unique and worthy.

Contents

Foreword

During covid 19, I was getting so many things to really think deeply and to know about that people, nature around me. My parents played an important role to always inspire me to write and think how does really this world run. I am sure that when people will read this book which include collection of the poetry and many more things which will help to relate it will their own life. I extremely enjoyed writting this book. My main credit goes to super power called God for always showing me new direction of my life and all my vedantu and school teachers and parents for their each single support and guidance.

Acknowledgements

The work on this book started in 2019. since then, a large number of teachers of Vedantu and my parents have made valuable suggestion and thoughts which i have felt and expressed in this writting work. Its not possible for me to acknowledge all of them individually but i take this opportunity to express my gratitude to them. specially to reach this position, i am wanting to thanks specially to entire vedantu team for all their effort in making my dream true by always motivating and encouraging me. without them and my parents i couldn't make it done. Finally i thank again from my core of heart to my parents(Mr. Sandeep kumar and Mrs. Dolly barnwal) for all their efforts and sacrifices for making my life wonderful.

1. A Parrot in the cage

A parrot came from a dense jungle,
He was looking so green and clever,
But never did any reprobation or bungle;
soon he was locked by man in the cage,
from that moment never be free as sage.
He thinks, he will enjoy to be with human,
but it was his biggest mistake to find trueman.
Life became so disappointed and painful ;
Nothing was there to survive in peaceful.
Cage was just like a closed box or jail,
and unable to take full breathe and be fail
. so difficult task to break the cage and fly,
Life was amazing but too difficult to fly in sky.
it was so difficult to say him, he is in freedom,
Again he was wanting to stay with his friends;
This time he doesn't want to live in any kingdom.
Its better to live alone but not in the cage,
life is not all about to be in a big palace
like parrot every person want to be engage.
Soon he started talking in human language
After some day he became an entertainment,
There were no any question to ask from himself
his life took a new turn as he started,
going to modern period to period ancient.
Never compare your life to anyone else,

because as it turns then ice also melts.

2. Why people always fight for wealth

People always fight for property and wealth,
don't know why they give more importance
even ready to loose life and sacrifice health.
Life is just like program or all about entertainment,
where people get chance to show their performance
just surviving this life isn't make any sense
making this life more beautiful by doing nice arrangement.
we know sometime it also make us face problem;
stop worrying and proving, its not any theorem.
sometimes its necessary to be sad and emotional,
but doesn't mean for that we have to be part of defence
and always try to be in the column of promotional.
In this world no one is in the favour of anyone,
you people will have to create your own history
every single people will be in favour of yours
when you will create your own history and won;
on that moment people will celebrate your victory.
No matter how you were bad or worst for them
only that people will hug you and tell you gem;
no one will behave like a rude or a stem.
As people cut it for its own profit and protection,
just doing chill and have patience quality,
you can handle anything by taking any kind of action.
in life always there is always chance and possibility.

3. Human and Tree

Sometime human also behave like a tree,
But one thing is that it never discriminate;
always ready to give oxygen but never disagree.
Both are dependent on each other,
Tree never refuse to share oxygen or do late;
they also bond a relationship with human
not like anyone else but just brother or sister.
Sometimes trees also fall and rise like superman
wothout tree no any human can stay alive
whether any plant or tree can surive.
Remorse, happiness all are the part of life,
Tree also feels pain when human kill from knife.
when tree smile, same way human also smiles.
There is no any life to survive without tree,
we all should leave it growing and be free.
Like human they also play in their own way,
seems as they feel energetic, they get sun ray.
As human do not look good in silent mode;
Tree also become silent when they removed from road.
Human can share their emotion and show problem,
trees can't do these thing but its peace emblem.
SAVE TREE SAVE EARTH

4. Dark night

Dark night with lighting star;
twinkling of star like a guitar.
No one makes noice like a day,
As many people move in the way.
Always wait for sweet dream;
while sleeping in a bed with pillow,
and scene of our home bulb as yellow.
All the trees become so silent,
only the moon is providing glorious light;
seems as he has many power and talent
which is in the colour of white.
And shining like a diamond so bright.
some of the stars dispersed in the sky,
which is far away from us and high.
Rotation of planets brings stars into view,
A glimmer of twilight enlivens the dew.

5. Childhood life

Lovely moment of the childhood,
No tension,no worry, no pressure
what and how to run our livelihood,
No school, no college, no homework,
always used to do our own work.
Playing, joking, eating was only our activites,
and getting new ideas and creativities.
Every child used to behave like a scientist,
when their toys used to fall and break
and mother used to make them listen to story
where there was a lot of fun and twist.
No child wants to lose their childhood,
but it is not in their hand,
every child also want to stood.
In the moment of the childhood,
no one knows about bad, better or good.
Best moment of our whole life,
who will not want to get it again
whether robber who kill people from knife.

6. Life may or may not be tough

Life may or may not be tough,
but it can not be so rough.
Always fix a weekly or daily goal,
try to achieve it and hit as a ball.
Trying again and again is the best
given up should not be an option,
and think high and have big dreams;
try making it true but never take rest.
Always try to put your hundred percent,
never think much about past and future
always look what happened in current.
Never think to build only the career,
try to put your name in the world history,
whether there is the cyclone or barrier.
Hardwork along with your smartwork,
will help you to reach till your dream
and it will let you come out from dark.

7. Maa

Nobody can do like mother,
mother never do like other.
Every person can cheat in life,
in the present of mother
no one can even touch or kill from knife.
In this world, there is no one any person;
who can take the place of mother,
own mother is much more better than stepmother
we can never pay mother loan,
mother can never do like unknown.
she is only the one who make us look the earth,
by keeping us nine month in her womb
and introduce ourself by giving birth.
by

8. Dedicated to father

Journey of daughter with father,
father always be so sweet to daughter.
He never refuse to give anything,
whether he has something or nothing.
Father is one only the person,
who always carry and take a lot of burden.
Father heart is always like a flower,
sweet, sensitive and has lot of power.
He always encourage his children and daughter,
to do something good in life as motivator.
experienced person for letting us know about universe
whether this or that thing is bad or worse.

9. Rhyme on family

People who lives in a family,
he or she always lives happily-happily
nothing is bigger than family.
family always be so lovely
family is precious gem given by God
It does not meet on the road.
Family means a festival of happiness,
we can not divide it into pieces.
Family always support in problem,
person who has a good family ,
He or she is lucky and solemn.

10. Transformer of my life

I had loose the hope of studying,
when the covid period was running.
But almighty sent Vedantu in my life,
who didn't let me loose my hope.
instead of losing hope,made me alive
All vedantu teachers behave like a parents,
and gives homework as the assignments
each teacher supported and motivated me,
whenever we want to study anything
they always be happy and do agree.
They all eraised from me phobia of maths
and also told me to move in right paths
one of the best thing, i experience in vedantu
All student get vedantu improvement promises,
best quality education and many test series.
Never expected things i got on vedantu
meaning of veda is knowledge, network is tantu.
Always be so grateful to three founders;
they are awesome teachers and innovator.
life became so cool to get this platform,
i get too many ideas and life changed as transform.
one of my hater subject became as lover called physics,
And got so many knowledge in the subject called civics.

11. Its farewell moment

Once you all were stranger for each other,
No one was knowing each other as brother or sister.
After sometime you all have dissolved yourself,
and became friends and going to stand in your life
with the help of teachers, parents and itself.
Instead of saying good bye, expressing good wishes,
life is the place where people will come and go,
Don't feel so emotional and walk too fast or slow.
Again you all are going to disperse from this school,
so don't be so tensioned in your life and be cool.
Now time has come to build your own career,
never get demotivate yourself whether there is barrier.
Never forget this school, teachers and junior;
we all are inspired from you and give respect as senior.
The door of the school is always open for you all,
whether you want any guidance or play with ball.
School life is the best example of learning,
now its time to go ahead in new turning.

12. Life after quarantine

Life after the quarantine,
better, best and fine
people will go on road
they will feel as they meet from God
Covid came in our nation;
it taught us a very big lesson.
From today, we will love creatures,
as well as we will give respect to nature.
we will get a amazing kind of freedom,
when we will go our school,
And there would so many funs as kingdom.
This twenty-twenty we will always remember;
one who comes in his under,
they people will have to live alone in chamber.

13. Our teacher

Teachers teach from nursery,
he tells that study is compulsory.
Teachers give lot of knowledge
from school till the college.
Teacher is a form of God,
He or she never wants that
i beat my students from rod.
Teachers are our guide,
No problem if he or she chide.
Teachers always want that
my student study more than me;
they never think my student sells tea.
Teachers always take student test,
they want to check whether they are good or best.
No knowledge without teacher
they always catches student weakness,
and teach them all about nature and creature.

14. Inspirational quotes

1. Life is such a gift that luck shines as soon as we open it.

2. If you have reached a peak in your life then don't be so happy because people don't even manage to reach and fall.

3. Just as a lotus blooms in mud but its petals be always so beautiful similarly, a good man and filled of good character man does not change his or her nature by staying in a bad company.

4. If you want to create history in your life then you have to break all the limitations of imagination.

5. Never be a part of those who become crowd in life, if you have to be it then be among those who make crowd that on seeing you and your achievement people get crowded.

6. Never judge yourself by marks or percentage, if you have to do it then do it on your hardwork, because in this universe each single person have unique quality.

7. If you want to enjoy in your life with full of happiness then for getting happiness you have to do hardwork and if you want that enjoyment and happiness in your life which no body has done in his life then you have to do those hardwork that nobody has done.

8. There is no hardwork in this world.just human beings make it difficult to speak but the one who doesn't think about all this. those people reach the destination.

9. More you ask question in your life, more you learn in your life. Its a fact of life.

10. I have often seen in my life that people who are poor, recognize themselves as well but when the same person reach on the higher

altitude of life then strangers also consider him/her as their own.

11. Never think of anything as small because that small things only helps us in getting into trouble.

12. I have learnt a great lesson from flowers in my own life that no matter how big situation comes, we should always let it go by bringing smile in our face.

13. Don't be so silent in life that people keep on speaking and you bear it.

14. In life, not only are the names of educated person, but the person who has good qualities and values.His/ her name is more than those who are educated.

15. Thinking about your goal and reaching that goal is the difference between sky and ground.

16. If you want happiness in your life then please try to distribute it thereafter, you see automatically happiness will come to you.

17. who does not have problems in life, but some people end up laughing on it, crying some.

18. In order to fly high in the life, our own dream is also to be high because unless we think of our dreams something big untill then we can't fly high.

19. Problems always teach us to become stronger and more stronger.

20. One thing in life must always remember that God only gives to the giver.

21. The bigger the goal in life, the bigger struggle you have to fight.

22. Everything in this world is precious before it is found and after it is lost.

23. you can make your life as big as you can think.

15. Noble profession of this world called medical and Life of doctors

Medical profession is one of the best profession in the world. In this career you get opportunity to serve the people and to understand their problems. It is also the toughest journey, where you have to bear many problems because patients can come anytime to you with their different-different kinds of diseases or problems and in that moment you can't ignore them whether its the climate of winter, summer or rain. No one knows whether that patient will survive or will die. At that moment Everything be in the hand of doctor and that duration always be a big challenge for doctors. This journey is so tough but one thing is special about them that doctors get lot of satisfaction. My aim is also to be senior cardiac surgeon of AIIMS Delhi and researcher in cancer. i chose this profession because i can't see people suffering from the health issues and i always try to think when some one lost his/her life that if i would be there then i could surely save him. I like to serve people, and to understand their problem and also love to communicate with them. There is a quote for medical aspirant that '' if you cannot wake for studying at the middle of night then how you will wake for save a life''. To be a sensitive person you can play the role of good human and only good human can be a good doctor. In this career you have to keep lot of patience and have to be lot of courage because when patient will come to you with their families and cry to save his/her life then in that moment you have to handle all these things because for that moment, you are only the hope for them and you can't sit quietly. For that moment you doctors have to do everything to save life. Generally I have seen people saying that " this or that doctor behaviour is very rude and he/she talks in bitter voice". No it is people's wrong understanding, i know that some of them might be rude but doctor generally behave like rude because untill if he/she will not behave like that then they can't treat patient because you would have been observed that doctors never treat or do all surgery kind of things to their family members because the reason is that from them they are emotionally, physically, mentally attached and they doctors can't do these kind of treatment to their closer ones. Doctors always worry about their patient health. I am so much excited to earn this position. In this journey you have to sacrifice lot of things and you have to learn many new-new words which will be totally different from the other and these all words you have to keep in mind always 24 hour. If you can't memorize these words, can't sacrifice things and can't work all day and night then its impossible for you. People say that medical education is lot of time consuming and i totally agree to them but we young minds have to think that when we will start saving people's life from getting die then nothing is bigger than it. You can understand when you will save someone life and later when you see smile on his/her face and on that moment people only indicate to you by saying that " This is only the one who could save my life and gave me one more opportunity to explore this world again". Now a days if we look people around us then most of them are losing their life by the severe condition of their health as example we can take that heart attack and cancer became as most common to the people and mainly from these kind of problem, people lose their life. I know that it is so tough to do but it suppose to be hard, if it would not be hard then everyone can do it but only the tough situation and difficulties make people unique or extraordinary from the others and it is going to worth it. Doctors are the second form of God in the earth. I have heard people saying that this or that doctor is so bad and he/she doesn't know anything because they couldn't save some life of the people. Don't judge any doctor by their treatment always look that how much effort they are putting to save life, we even can't take our imagination there. So medical profession is one of the most toughest one. I always follow a quote " i am not here to only make my career but here to create history and to be an example for the world" but one thing always put me in big situation that in this profession you can't spend time with your family because at any moment you can get a call for emergency and in that moment you have to decide whether you want to spend time with your family or who are going to be ready to go the hospital and save life of the people.People around us always say one slogan" Jai javan, jai kisan and jai vigyan but i too belive in this slogan that" jai javan, jai kisan, jai chikitshak(doctor) and jai vigyan". We can do anything in our life but when our health will be good. Every single work is dependent on the health. we must always give more priority to our health and to always respect doctors because to be in a small operation theatre and putting all life in risk without having meal is really very hectic and tough and all also respect to our future doctor who is going to come out with different ideas to make people's life more comfortable and longer.

16. Turning point of my life

Once upon a time there was a moment in which my life had totally turned in new direction. When i was in 9th or since childhood my aim is to be a senior cardiac surgeon of AIIMS Delhi and want to research in cancer. Till 8th-9th grade no one was knowing about my career that i want to pursue my career in medicine. Everything was running smoothly. There were two or three teachers in vedantu as their name was Bornali mam and Raina mam whom i told about my aimbition and they are only the one who started motivating me and supporting me by calling me as Dr.Aashi. I was studying in India's biggest online learning platform ''Vedantu'' because there were no any good coaching institute in my village. One day i attempted one exam called VOTE in vedantu and then through schlorship i joined it. By the awesome teachers help and guidance i was getting so much of knowledge and started my preparation for NEET foundation. One day i knew about one other institute entrance test then i decided to attempt it for testing myself. On the exam day i was fearing a lot that it was my first national level test. Thereafter i increased my confidence and attempted it. thereafter when result came out i am both happy and sad respectively because happy because i had qualifed that test and sad because i hadn't get good rank as per my expectation and for that moment i became so discouraged and disappointed then when i shared about this news to my vedantu teachers who are so amazing, mindblowing etc. They again motivated me and after some day i started getting too much call from that institute for admission but i was not wanting to join other institute by leaving Vedantu because it was and still is God gift for me. One night i got called from some other institute by saying that you have been selected in top 10 student list of jharkhand and after listening this news i was just feeling like if i hadn't attempted any exam then how it could be possible to get selected among these students. The man from the institute was saying to me that they are coming to take my interview at my home so, parents were also getting joy of tears when they listen the things and that night i went to my parents asking about my career decision and as they asked me that " beta whats your further plan about your career" i replied to them that mumma and papa i already chose medicine for my further studies then they were like beta its time consuming education so plz try to make your career in engineering and wanting me to do aerospace engineering from IIT bombay as it was also my dream because i was the girl for that moment who was wanting to make my career in so many fields and i had also interest in space science but my dream was AIIMS only so i told my parents that in 11th i will choose both maths and biology and i will prepare for both the exams but taking both subject i had picked up big risk because to manage both biology and maths are so difficult but since childhood, i always use to think that by taking risk only people be unique and different from the others. Next day when interviewer came in my home. i was also happy because it was my first interview. Everything was going smoothly, when interviewer started asking me question and i became so nervous and scared and was unable to answer any of his question even although i was knowing each single answer but for that moment i had became totally blanked and nothing to answer but that guy told me to be calm down and don't panic but for that moment i was just thinking that now i can't do anything but literally i am so thankful to God that interviewer told me that this was not your main interview as i will give you some question to solve so he sent me into another room with his laptop and gave 10 questionwithin the timing of 15 minutes and i was just amazed to hear from him the word "congratulations" because in that question i got 8 out of 10 and 80% schlorship and in that moment i was just full of joy tears and mood had totally changed within 1 hours and i was just feeling so relaxed and calm and from that moment i decided to take both biology and maths and finally parents got agree that, okay i can choose medicine for my career.

Moral of this story- We should always try to take risk in life to make our career better from the others and failure always bring success and happiness from the other side. The main work we should do is to be calm down and keep patience. A single exam hour can change your entire life decision but only you have to keep faith in God and parents.